25

PRIMARY SOURCES
★★★★★★★★★★★★★★★★★★★ OF ★★★★★★★★★★★★★★★★★★★
IMMIGRATION AND MIGRATION
★ IN AMERICA ★

IMMIGRATION AND THE SLAVE TRADE

Africans Come to America
(1607–1830)

Jeremy Thornton

The Rosen Publishing Group's

PowerKids Press™

PRIMARY SOURCE

New York

For Danny Thornton, my father

Published in 2004 by The Rosen Publishing Group, Inc.
29 East 21st Street, New York, NY 10010

First Edition

Editor: Rachel O'Connor
Book Design: Emily Muschinske
Book Layout: Mike Donnellan, Eric DePalo

Photo Credits: Cover and title page The Sheridan Libraries of The John Hopkins University; p. 4 Library of Congress Geography and Map Division; p. 7 © Corbis; pp. 8 (left), 11 (center) Library of Congress Rare Book and Special Collections Division; p. 8 (top right) The Mariners' Museum, Newport News, Virginia; p. 8 (bottom right) Picture Collection, The Branch Libraries, New York Public Library, Astor, Lenox and Tilden Foundations; p. 11 (top) © North Wind Picture Archives; p. 11 (bottom) Courtesy of the Gene Alexander Peters Collection; pp. 12, 15 (top), 20 (bottom) Library of Congress Prints and Photographs Division; p. 15 (bottom) Culver Pictures; p. 16 Stratford Historical Society, Stratford, Connecticut; p. 19 (top) © National Maritime Museum, London; p.19 (bottom) The Library of Virginia; p 20 (top) The Library Company of Philadelphia.

Thornton, Jeremy, 1973–
Immigration and the slave trade : Africans come to America (1607–1830) / Jeremy Thornton.— 1st ed.
     v. cm. — (Primary sources of immigration and migration in America)
Includes bibliographical references (p.) and index.
Contents: A forced migration — Africans in America — African slaves — The terrible voyage — Arriving in America — The occupations of a slave — The life of a slave — The legalization of slavery — A merging of cultures — Slavery ends.
ISBN 0-8239-6829-4 (lib. bdg.) — ISBN 0-8239-8955-0 (pbk.)
1. African Americans—History—Juvenile literature. 2. Africans—Migrations—History—Juvenile literature. 3. Slaves—United States—History—Juvenile literature. 4. Slave trade—United States—History—Juvenile literature. 5. Slave trade—Africa—History—Juvenile literature. 6. Africa—Emigration and immigration—History—Juvenile literature. 7. United States—Emigration and immigration—History—Juvenile literature. [1. African Americans—History. 2. Slavery—History. 3. Slave trade—History. 4. Africa—Emigration and immigration—History. 5. United States—Emigration and immigration—History.] I. Title. II. Series.
E185 .T465 2004
306.3'62'0973—dc21
                              2002155190

Manufactured in the United States of America

Contents

GVINEA propria, nec non NIGRITIÆ vel Terræ NIGRORVM maxima pars, Geographis hodiernis dicta utraq ÆTHIOPIA INFERIOR, à lujus quidem pars australis in delineationibus Auxilianis itineri Guineensi D. de Marchais insertis secundum Typos projectionis Aërographicæ Hassianæ designatæ & edita studio & labore Homannianorum Hæredum Norimb. cum Privil. S.C.M. A 1743.

La GVINEE de meme que la plus grande Partie du Pais des NEGRES, appellée par les Geographes modernes ETHIOPIE INFERIEVRE à meridionale, tirées des nouveaux geographiques de Mr. d'Anville, qu'il a insérez au Voyage du Chev. de Marchais, & puis dressées suivant les Loix de la nouvelle projection de feu Mr. le Prof. Has, par les Heritiers d'Homann A. 1743.

ZARÆ
ZANHAGA. DESERTVM MAXIMVM
DESERTI BARBARIÆ quod MARE SABULOSUM dicitur

ÆTHIOPIA
INFERIOR vel ANTERIOR
TOMBVT TOCRVR
LAMLEM
BAMBARA POP.
TERRA NIGRITARVM
INCOGNITA et ut volunt DESERTA
NIGRORVM

R. DAHOME DAUMA
sub quo ABDRA et JUDA
GUINEA
PROPRIA
ÆTHIO
SUPERIOR
PIAE
SVPERIORIS
SEPTEM MONTES
R. MAJOMBA
BAKE-BAKE
GABON PONGO REGNVM
ORIS
PARS INFER.

OCEANVS
ÆTHIOPIOVS

Meridies

A Forced Migration

Many of the early immigrants who landed on American shores came in search of a better life. Some came to take advantage of the many resources available. Others came for religious and political freedom. However, most early immigrants did not come by choice. Over a period of about 300 years, more than 10 million Africans were forced from their homelands to North America and South America to become slaves.

The Portuguese were the first Europeans to bring African slaves to the Americas in the mid-1500s. They forced the Africans to work on the sugar plantations in their colonies in South America.

Slavery in Africa was not based on the idea that whites were the masters and that blacks were the slaves. Such racism only developed when the black Africans were brought to America and to other parts of the world.

Africans in America

European nations such as England and Spain began to colonize sections of North America in the early seventeenth century. They found that they did not have enough people to work the vast areas of land they now owned. One solution was to buy enslaved Africans. The first boatload of African slaves arrived on the East Coast of North America in 1619. A Dutch ship landed at Jamestown, Virginia, carrying a human cargo of 20 Africans.

Slavery had existed in Africa before the colonies were formed. However, in Africa, many of the slaves were treated more like indentured servants.

The Dutch ship that arrived in Jamestown in 1619 had gained its cargo of black Africans after it had captured a Spanish slave ship. The Africans were sold to colonists, marking the beginning of the trans-Atlantic slave trade.

Olaudah Equiano;
or
GUSTAVUS VASSA,
the African?

Published March 1 1789 by G. Vassa

Trinkets worn as Spells. p. 45.

Gold Hatband

Gold Horn

Necklace

Arm-Ring

Hair-Combs

When European ships arrived on the coast of Africa, they brought with them metal goods to trade for the slaves.

Olaudah Equiano was sold into slavery as a child. After gaining his freedom, Equiano wrote his autobiography in 1789.

African Slaves

In Africa, slaves sometimes worked for powerful rulers or kings. However, many of the Africans exiled to America had not been slaves at all. Some were prisoners of war. Others were kidnapped from their homes and were sold to slave merchants. Some were criminals who were forced into slavery as punishment for their crimes.

The Africans who were forced to go to America came from a land rich in its ethnic and religious cultures. Africa was made of many countries with thousands of different languages. The Africans had many different religions and believed in many gods.

African merchants kidnapped possible slaves from the Africa interior and forced them to walk in "slave caravans" to European forts on the coast. Chained and starved, many of the Africans did not survive the journey.

The Terrible Voyage

The enslaved Africans bound for America were herded like cattle onto ships. Often, they did not know where they were being taken. Then the terrible journey across the Atlantic, called the Middle Passage, would begin. The Africans were thrown together below deck, were chained, and were given little to eat. Sometimes they were packed so tightly that some of them suffocated. There were no bathrooms. Many of the slaves became sick. Those who were ill were sometimes thrown overboard to keep the other slaves from becoming sick. The slave traders wanted to arrive with as many healthy slaves as they could.

The Europeans built forts to house slaves and goods before they were loaded onto boats. These forts were located along Africa's coast, near ports. The slave fort passageway was often the point of no return for many Africans.

A diagram of the lower deck of a slave ship shows how tightly the African men, women, and children were packed together.

Onboard the ships, the African men were chained in pairs, wrist to wrist or ankle to ankle, with shackles.

This slave auction block can be seen today off Route 728 in Campbell County, Virginia.

This slave pen in Alexandria, Virginia, held hundreds of slaves headed for New Orleans to be sold.

TO BE SOLD, on board the Ship *Bance-Island*, on tuesday the 6th of *May* next, at *Ashley-Ferry*, a choice cargo of about 250 fine healthy

NEGROES,

just arrived from the Windward & Rice Coast. —The utmost care has already been taken, and shall be continued, to keep them free from the least danger of being infected with the SMALL-POX, no boat having been on board, and all other communication with people from *Charles-Town* prevented.

Austin, Laurens, & Appleby.

N. B. Full one Half of the above Negroes have had the SMALL-POX in their own Country.

Arriving in America

Once the slave ships arrived on the East Coast of America, the slaves would be sold to agents or dealers. The agent could offer each slave at a fixed price, could bargain on the price, or could run an auction. The African men, women, and children were poked and examined roughly by the dealers. The slaves were usually tired and confused after weeks of being held captive on the ships. They were not used to such treatment, especially those who were of high social standing in their homeland. After the sale, the dealers would transport, or move, the slaves inland and sell them to farmers and plantation owners.

This 1780s advertisement to sell slaves assures readers that the slaves from this ship have not been infected with the deadly smallpox.

The Occupations of a Slave

Most of the African slaves brought to America were needed for work on the huge plantations in the southern colonies, such as those in South Carolina. Slavery also existed in farming regions farther north, such as the colonies of New York and New Jersey.

Once sold, slaves were often branded with hot irons to identify them if they tried to escape. The slaves on plantations were forced to work on the land from dawn until dusk, taking orders from a supervisor. They were not paid, and they were beaten if the work was not done properly. Slaves on the smaller farms in the north usually worked alongside their owners in the fields. Some performed chores in the house or the barn.

Right: In this 1858 wood engraving, African slaves are shown picking cotton on a plantation in Georgia.

Below: Many African slaves had come from rice-producing regions of Africa, and therefore had the skills that were needed to grow rice successfully.

DITCHING

REAPING

This drawing is called Flora. It is believed to be of a 19-year-old black woman who was sold into slavery in 1796 in Connecticut. It is most likely the earliest identifiable slave image in America. The drawing was accompanied by this bill of sale (right), whereby Asa Benjamin purchased Flora for the sum of 25 pounds.

The Life of a Slave

Owners were able to beat, brand, or even kill slaves mostly without fear of punishment. The colonists viewed the slaves as property. They were therefore free to treat slaves as they pleased. Slaves were not allowed to decide where they wanted to live or what they wanted to do. They could be sold at any time to another owner. Sometimes this meant that a slave was separated from his or her family, even if the family had managed to stay together so far.

There was very little comfort in the lives of the slaves. What comfort they did find came from other slaves, from their religion, and from their shared beliefs. They made it through the terrible days by supporting one another.

The Legalization of Slavery

Slavery first became legal in Massachusetts in 1641. In the next few years, Connecticut and Virginia also legally recognized slavery. By 1750, all 13 of the British colonies in North America had legalized slavery. The number of slaves brought from Africa to European colonies in America increased partly because of a law that was passed by Parliament in Great Britain in 1698. It stated that any subject of Britain could trade in slaves. The number of slaves being transported on British ships jumped from 5,000 annually in the late 1600s to 45,000 by the middle of the next century. However, because of the terrible conditions on these ships, usually about one-third of the Africans died during the trip.

Right: *This is the coat of arms of the South Sea Company, a British company which was founded in 1711 in order to trade in slaves with Spanish America.*

Below: *In 1682, Virginia's General Assembly passed an act that stated that "all servants imported into this country are hereby deemed and taken to be slaves."*

A Merging of Cultures

By the 1750s, African slaves were beginning to form attachments to America, despite the hardships they endured. They slowly began to accept America as their home. Some began to accept Christianity as their religion, finding comfort in the Bible, with its messages of freedom and equality. They maintained a sense of their African heritage through their music. Music was one way in which slaves could keep a sense of themselves and of their honor, in spite of the mistreatment they suffered. The blues and jazz music of today are examples of the music that came from a mix of African and European roots.

Juliann Jane Tillman was one of the preachers of the African Methodist Episcopal (AME) Church in Philadelphia. Inset: Richard Allen established the Bethel AME Church in Philadelphia in 1794. Allen was born a slave.

Slavery Ends

Ever since the first slaves were brought to America, the morality of slavery was questioned. By the end of the 1700s, these questions of morality became louder and more frequent. There was often conflict in America between those who supported slavery and those who opposed it. In 1807, Congress took the first step toward outlawing slavery by passing a law that banned the bringing in of slaves. The conflict over slavery eventually led to the Civil War. President Abraham Lincoln officially freed all slaves in the Confederate states when he issued the Emancipation Proclamation in 1863. However, it took many years before blacks acquired rights that were equal to those of white Americans.

Glossary

attachments (uh-TACH-mints) Connections to something or someone.

auction (OK-shun) A sale at which goods are sold to whoever pays the most.

cargo (KAR-goh) The goods carried by an airplane, a ship, or a truck.

Civil War (SIH-vul WOR) The war fought between the Northern and Southern states of America from 1861 to 1865.

Confederate states (kun-FEH-duh-ret STAYTS) States that fought for the South during the Civil War.

Emancipation Proclamation (ih-man-sih-PAY-shun prah-kluh-MAY-shun) A paper, signed by Abraham Lincoln during the Civil War, that freed all slaves held in Southern territory.

exiled (EG-zyld) To have been made to leave one's home or country.

heritage (HER-ih-tij) The cultural traditions passed from parent to child.

immigrants (IH-muh-grints) People who move to a new country from another country.

indentured servants (in-DEN-churd SER-vints) People who have worked for another person for a fixed amount of time for payment of travel or living costs.

resources (REE-sors-es) Things that occur in nature and that can be used or sold, such as gold, coal, or wool.

suffocated (SUH-fuh-kayt-ed) Died from a lack of air.

supervisor (SOO-per-vy-zer) A person who manages and directs work or workers.

Index

Primary Sources

Cover. Insurrection on board a slave ship. Reproduced from William Fox's *A Brief History of the Wesleyan Missions n the West Coast of Africa,* 1851. **Page 4.** Map extending from present-day Senegal and Gambia in the northwest, and to Gabon in the southwest. Hand-colored, engraved map. 1743. The inset shows the dress, dwellings, and work of some Africans. **Page 8. Left.** Detail from the title page of Oloudah Equiano's autobiography, *The Interesting Narrative of the Life of Olaudah Equiano or Gustavus Vassa the African.* Eighth edition, 1794. **Bottom right.** Slave caravans on the road. Reproduced from *The Boy Travellers on the Congo,* by Thomas Wallace Knox. 1888. **Page 11.** Gate of no return. Passage into a slave fort. The Mariner's Museum. Newport News, Virginia. **Top Left.** Diagram of a slave ship. Circa 1790. Shows the lower deck of a slave ship with African bodies packed together for transport to America. **Center inset.** Leg shackles used to restrict slaves. Woodcut by Samuel Wood. 1807. **Page 12. Left.** Interior of a slave pen in Alexandria City, Virginia. Medford Historical Society. **Top.** Slave auction block. Green Hill plantation in Campbell County, Virginia. **Right.** Newspaper advertisement advertising the sale of enslaved Africans on board the ship Bance Island. 1780s. **Page 15. Top.** African slaves on a cotton plantation in Georgia. Woodcut. 1858. **Page 16.** *Flora* and bill of sale. December 13, 1796. The silhouette, which accompanied the bill of sale, is believed to be the first identifiable image of a slave in America. Flora was purchased by Asa Benjamin of Stratford, Connecticut, from Margaret Dwight in New Haven. **Page 19.** Act passed by the General Assembly of the colony of Virginia that stated all non-Christian servants brought into the country would be taken as slaves. 1682. **Inset.** South Sea Company coat of arms. 1711. A slave trading company. **Page 20.** Mrs. Juliann Jane Tillman, preacher of the A.M.E. Church. Lithograph. 1844. Printed Peter S. Duvall. Drawn by Alfred Hoffy. **Inset.** Bethel African Methodist Church, Philadelphia. Early 1800s. Established by Richard Allen, born a slave, it was the first church organized and directed by blacks in the United States.

Web Sites

Due to the changing nature of Internet links, PowerKids Press has developed an online list of Web sites related to the subject of this book. This site is updated regularly. Please use this link to access the list:

www.powerkidslinks.com/psima/strade/